RESIDUAL INCOME MAGIC

A Proven Roadmap for an Ongoing Stream of Residual
Income that Provides an Amazing Lifestyle, Time
Freedom, and the Life Most Only Dream About

JERRIKA COX

WIFI WEALTH
www.wifiwealth.com

ISBN: 978-0-578-94774-7

Cover design by David James

Printed in the United States of America

ACKNOWLEDGMENTS

We have learned to be grateful for so many things on this journey and gratefulness has become one of the driving forces in our lives and business. We always teach about the importance of gratefulness, and strive to live it out for both ourselves and for those around us.

I would like to thank my mentor, Clint Jameson, for making this book and our business possible. Without Clint's insights and guidance we might have struggled for many more years dreaming about what might be possible for us and for the world that we wanted to impact.

I would also like to thank all of our clients who have put their faith and trust in us to help them change their lives in so many positive ways. It is such a joy and pleasure to serve all of you. You are all so amazing! Every morning Brycen and I wake up happy and full of joy knowing that we can continue to help people just like those reading this book right now.

Jerrika Cox

CONTENTS

INTRODUCTION
A PERSONAL NOTE FROM JERRIKA

"If you do not find a way to make money while you sleep, you will work until you die."

— Warren Buffet

Are you tired of living a life where you work for someone else rather than yourself? Do you want to have the freedom to do whatever you want whenever you want, but don't know how to get there?

Residual income is something that many would like to have, but most don't think it's possible to get or they don't know how to get started. Those who have tried and failed did so because they didn't get the right guidance from an expert who knows what he's talking about.

This book will give you all the tools you need so that by the time you finish reading this book, your mind will be set on making residual income happen for yourself. And you'll know exactly what to do. This book, *Residual Income Magic*, reveals the secret success strategies that most so-called experts will never share.

The idea of leaving the 9 to 5 work environment and achieving financial independence online has only been a dream for many people. However, with a little hard work and dedication, it can become a reality for you. In this book you will learn how to quit your job and make money from home, entirely on autopilot, without any boss or schedule telling you what to do. If your goal is simply to add additional income *without* leaving your job, then this book will help you with that too. If you're an entrepreneur already making money online and want to take your income and business to the next level you've also come to the right place.

Do you ever wish you could work less and make more? That's the goal most people have, but it's tough to do when your life revolves around a 9 to 5 job. If this sounds like you, then I have some good news! You can live the lifestyle you want with residual income — and even make money while you sleep. It all starts by learning the insider secrets for living the residual income lifestyle that many people don't know about. We're so excited that you made the decision to get your hands on a copy of this FREE (pay only for shipping and handling book). I'm passionate about helping anyone who has the desire to succeed.

If you're willing to spend some time to carefully study this book...If you're willing to keep an open mind about what we have to offer...If you're willing follow the suggestions and if you're willing to explore this further, then by taking the next steps you will have the opportunity to move away from a life of not-enough-income, of too much stress in doing what you are presently doing, to a life of financial freedom. You'll be able to do what you want to do, when you want to do it — and you can have great success.

With your success in mind,
Jerrika Cox
Wifi Wealth

CHAPTER 1

WHY I WROTE THIS BOOK

"Achievement happens when we pursue and attain what we want.
Success comes when we are in clear pursuit of why we want it"
— Simon Sinek

Keep Simon Sinek's quote in mind when it comes to your own success in life. If you have a strong enough reason why, then you can succeed at anything. We succeeded because we had a strong enough reason why — the same reason that motivated us to write this book.

For years we struggled to live the life we dreamed about. We hit dead end after dead end. At one point we were even broke. But we were determined even though we often woke up in a cold sweat in the middle of the night with a deep fear of success and the prospect of what we would do with all that money that we wanted to make.

At the same time negative thoughts kept coming back. And people were constantly telling us "there is no way you can do this" — which only made matters worse. With initial failure after failure, we looked at each other thinking, "Can we really, really do this?" And worse yet, we spent millions of dollars and many years trying to figure out what would work. But to tell the truth, what kept me "keeping on" was that I didn't want to be on my death bed looking back thinking I wisha wisha I had hung in a little longer to live the lifestyle I knew I deserved.

We did know one thing for sure — success leaves clues. So for every waking moment over the course of eight years, we lived and breathed learning about the world of Internet marketing success. We also did what turned out to be a smart thing as I look back: rather than thinking we could get all the answers on our own, we surrounded ourselves with knowledgeable experts and, more importantly, people who had maintained that positive attitude we all need in order to massively succeed. Finally we discovered the success secrets and made millions of dollars.

We also wanted to help others like you. but initially we hit a brick wall. Why? Because the systems we applied for ourselves could take others months and months, if not years and years, to implement. The problem was that many of the so-called Internet marketing experts don't want to cut to the chase and give you simple-to-follow answers. Some of them are more intent on selling the next program and filling their own pockets rather than helping you succeed. We felt that this just isn't fair, so we've leveled the playing field by providing the requisite information, a system, and an approach that can work for anyone. There's also so much darn information available about all of these so-called opportunities that it can quickly get very confusing for most people.

Because our system is easy, as I'll explain later, we often thought that we should call this system "ISFAP" which stands for "Internet Success for Any Person." Instead, we decided to call our book *Residual Income Magic*...and I have to tell you that many of our clients do call it "magic."

The magic part is that anyone can go from "not enough money", "too much stress," "yearning for but not achieving the dream," to the life we all want deep down inside. Our system can do that for most people who have the right attitude and a willingness to learn.

As it has been for us, another magic part of this system has nothing to do with money. It has to do with having the resources to help others like we have done. We've helped others in many ways because we had the time to do so. For example, I mentor former drug addicts and alcoholics. I can't put a value on helping others in that way. There has been no greater feeling for us than the comfort and security that comes with financial freedom. We want to provide the opportunity for that feeling to as many people as possible.

Exercises

"Without reflection, we go blindly on our way, creating more unintended consequences, and failing to achieve anything useful."
— Margaret J. Wheatley

In this section I shared with you the reason why I wrote this book. I also mentioned the importance of having a strong reason "why." What's your reason for why you are pursuing a residual income opportunity with the hope of seeing success? Please take some time to answer ALL the questions below. A better life, a better future for you and your loved ones is at stake.

- How would having your own Internet business with an ongoing stream of residual income make you feel?

- If you had an ongoing stream of residual income and someone were to observe your life, what would they see?

- If you were to tell me what your new life was like what do you imagine that you would say?

- What would it be like each morning to wake up knowing that you had your own business and an ongoing stream of residual income?

- What would your family think about what you are doing if you were fully able to take care of their financial needs?

- If you have kids, what lesson do you think you would be teaching them as they saw you with your own Internet residual income business?

- What would it be like having the time and freedom to do what you want to do when you want to do it?

- If you could take a vacation anywhere in the world, where would you go?

- How would you help others if you had both the time and money to do that?

- If you had this freedom and financial situation, what would you do differently that you are not doing now?

- If you left your current job with this new life, what would you tell your boss?

- How would you feel if you left your current job today to go on to your new life?

- What other questions should I be asking you here that I did not?

If the answers to any of these questions completely confirmed in your mind that you want the residual lifestyle and that you would do anything and everything to get that, then I can genuinely say "congratulations" on the change in your life, in your business, in your world that is about to happen for you. I'm so excited for you. Keep reading and let's begin your journey to a residual income-filled life!

CHAPTER 2
THE RESIDUAL LIFESTYLE

What is residual income?

In the context of income, residual income refers to income received after the income-producing work has been completed (also called "passive income" or "recurring income"). Rental income, income from real estate, interest and dividend income are examples of residual income. Your residual income comes after you have made a profit from your online business. A profitable business could, for instance, begin by opening a Shopify store. Getting the business going will take some time and effort. There is usually very little work required after the initial effort to maintain residual income.

What our clients tell us
(We felt the same way)

"Long ago, I realized that success leaves clues, and that people who produce outstanding results do specific things to create those results. I believed that if I precisely duplicated the actions of others, I could reproduce the same quality of results that they had."

– Tony Robbins

We love hearing from our clients — people just like you.

Here is what a few of our clients have said once we've helped them successfully achieve the residual income lifestyle:

"Earning residual income seemed so complicated. There were so many choices, and it seemed like doing this would take lots of time. I was confused and ready to give up until I got Jerrika's book" — **Gennifer W.**

"Jerrika's partner Brycen cares so much. He's the real deal. It seems like there is nothing he won't do to help people live a better life. In his personal life, it shows. Brycen volunteers his time each week to help recovering drug addicts and alcoholics." — **Brian E.**

"I dreamed for years about earning money on autopilot every month but thought that could never happen for me. When I got Jerrika's book I couldn't put it down. I'm so excited about what the future holds for us!" — **Bennett M.**

Look, I don't know your situation. I don't know if you're casually interested in earning residual income or not. If you have already firmly decided to make living the residual lifestyle a reality, no matter what, then you can skip this chapter. However, if you are just thinking about it, I want to share why people like you have purchased this book with some of them ultimately becoming our clients.

I'm sharing this because it might help you to further consider the reasons why you might want to get totally serious and take massive action to get the residual income life you want and deserve (whether you get help from us our not). Many people tell us that they want to leave their 9 to 5 jobs for the following reasons:

- **They need more time with family**. When you're working a 9 to 5 job, it can be hard to find time for family. One of the most important things in life is spending quality time with your loved ones. You need them when you're struggling and they will always be there for you when you need them the most. When times are tough, we all need someone who loves us unconditionally and whom we love just as much right back! Spending some quality time with those people every day should be something that we all strive for because it makes life so much better!

- **The environment is toxic to them.** You may not realize it, but your job is just as important to your mental health as it is to your physical health. A toxic work environment can leave you feeling drained both physically and mentally, and this ultimately causes stress and anxiety. Leaving a toxic work environment will allow you to lead a more fulfilling life outside of the office. Having a successful online Internet business can take anyone from "I hate my job" to "I love my life."

- **They're dissatisfied with their present position/ responsibilities.** Sitting at your desk day in and day out can have a negative impact on you. In fact, an estimated 40% of people who work full-time are dissatisfied with their jobs. But why does this happen?[1]

There are a number of reasons that contribute to job dissatisfaction, including long hours, poor pay and benefits, lack of advancement opportunities, or simply not liking the company culture. You may also be feeling down because you don't feel challenged enough by your position anymore or you may find that it has become too routine for you.

It's important to recognize these feelings so that you can take steps towards improving them before they negatively affect your mental health even more than they already have! Having a successful Internet business is about much more than the money that will come. Great mental health will come too! And who can put a dollar value on that one?

- **They are sick and tired of the daily commute.** A long daily commute can be very demoralizing, costly in terms of both time and money, and hazardous to your mental health. It's important to find ways to reduce your commute as much as possible so that you can live a happier life!

  If you're looking for a career change or just want an additional income stream, you should consider taking advantage of the many online platforms that allow you to work remotely full-time without ever having to leave home again! Some companies are even hiring remote workers on 100% commission, meaning that the only thing holding you back is how much effort you put into your success.

- **They feel they are underpaid in their current job.** Their present employer pays comparatively low wages relative to their the level of responsibility and they don't feel that it's worth the cost of commuting every day for such a meager paycheck that barely covers the bills and household expenses.

Meanwhile, the economy is booming with many companies raking in large profits and yet, employees aren't seeing a corresponding increase in their salary.

In fact, many are working overtime without any pay at all. Why? The reason is simple: companies underpay their workers because they must remain competitive with other companies that won't be paying their employees higher wages. It's a cycle of poverty that has been going on for years. This is why you need to consider moving out on your own so that you can earn the money you deserve. That makes sense doesn't it?

- **Their boss is an idiot and they want to do something else.** "The average worker spends close to 40 hours per week in a workplace. That's more than half your waking life and probably the last place you want to spend it if you're not getting satisfaction from what you do." "And yet, most people — even those who are successful at their jobs — think that their bosses are idiots."[2] "Why is this? Why would we put up with such an ungrateful attitude towards our hard work?" "If your job isn't making you happy, then why stay there?" There is another way. I guess that may be one reason why you decided to get this book.

- **They hate their job.** According to the Bureau of Labor

Statistics, as many as 80% of U.S. workers are not engaged at work and nearly 50% are "actively disengaged."[3] In an interview, motivational speaker Tony Robbins said, "Most people think they can't do anything about their situation." Based on my experience and that of my clients, that simply isn't true.

- **It's just too toxic to your well-being to fear an impending layoff.** Tony Robbins says, "the most important decision you will ever make is whether to be a victim or a survivor."[4] This is powerful advice and something that can't be overstated. It's not just about surviving — it's about thriving!

The same goes for your career. You might fear an impending layoff during your career, but what if it were actually an opportunity? What if this fear of layoff could give you the chance to find out more about who you are as an individual?

There's no time like the present to start planning for your next move, so let's talk today.

By the way, if you think a layoff couldn't happen to you, here are some shocking facts: A layoff or firing happens to most people at some point during their career. The number one reason is because they can't keep up with the fast pace of work in today's world. The second most common reason for a layoff or firing is due to an organizational restructuring, which means that the company needs to get rid of some positions so they can focus on what really matters. A third reason you might be let go from your job is because you are not meeting performance expectations and have been put on notice before being fired.

Do any of these reasons resonate with you? If so, your decision to get this book now was a smart one. Getting the book is an important first step to not letting a job loss mess up your life and your dreams.

Why many people need a second income

More than ever, many people are seeking additional income and, specifically, an ongoing stream of residual income. According to Money Magazine, "44 million Americans have a side hustle."[5] Reasons vary but some of the key reasons include:[6]

- **A less stable job environment.** The pandemic has resulted in a reshuffling of many jobs and the introduction of requirements for new skills that many people don't have. Many who are dealing with these issues (whether currently employed or not) seek additional income through an online business as a form of financial security insurance.

  Remote work, combined with the growth of the Internet as a platform for home businesses, has awakened many people to the huge possibilities of a second income. The felt-need for a second income has been stimulated by the actual opportunity for a second income.

- **A greater understanding of the importance of financial**

management. According to the Board of Standards, "the primary reason that clients visit financial planners is to discuss their financial concerns which include: preparing for retirement, managing and reducing debt, building an emergency fund, building a college fund, saving for a home purchase or renovation, sheltering income from taxes, generating retirement income, providing for future medical needs, and, if there is money left, figuring out how to vacation or travel more." The report goes on to say that "47% of consumers are technically classified as 'troubled' and they are worried about debt. Another 30% are 'somewhat' troubled with debt, and 23% are not at all concerned about their debts."[7]

- **Be-Your-Own-Boss Trends**. More and more people want to be their own bosses. This has indirectly driven the desire for a second income. When the need for a second income is satisfied, then those who have it can feel more secure about their monthly income, less concerned about losing a job, and more confident about what the future holds. Having that second income will make it easier to achieve your financial goals.

  Another benefit of a second income is it makes it more likely that a person will be able to retire early. Having that second income also allows for financial diversification — meaning there is less risk if one of the income sources dries up.

Meet the residual lifestyle

"Rich people believe 'I create my life.' Poor people believe 'Life happens to me.'"

– Harv Eker

You've probably heard of many people who have left their job so that they can do what they want to do when they want to do it. You've heard of those who get the income they want, and achieve the freedom to do what they want, when they want, and much more. You may now be wondering what it would be like to leverage the power of what we call "residual income magic." Well, strap on your seat belt and let me share with you what it will be like...

It's not every day that you hear about the residual income lifestyle. It might sound like a dream come true, but what does it mean to actually live this way? The idea of living off of money that you've earned online is intriguing to many people. After all, who wouldn't want to just work one job and make money from home? In this book we're going to explore what it means for someone who has chosen to live the residual income lifestyle.

When you are living the residual income lifestyle you can:

- **Make money while you sleep**. You're probably wondering what it's like to make money while you sleep from an Internet business. Well, I can tell you that the best part is waking up every morning and seeing how much work was done on your behalf overnight. You'll be amazed at how easy it is to start making money in a completely passive way once you know the right strategies.

The internet lifestyle is the future and it's closer than you think! Keep reading to learn more and you'll understand why owning a business online WILL give you freedom from any job where computers might replace humans someday soon (even if not tomorrow). And then there's retirement the traditional way — "working" until you're six feet under. That isn't really the way to go, is it?

- **Make additional income while working your regular job**. One of our clients emailed us and said this, "I was at the end of my rope, working a job I abhorred. My boss yelled at me constantly and I dreaded going to work every day. One Friday evening after coming home from another long shift, I told my wife that I couldn't take it anymore — that's when she shared this book with me. I had never heard of Internet businesses before but as soon as she explained how they worked and what people were doing with them, I got excited about our future."

- **Enjoy passive income for the rest of your life**. I know what you're thinking: What's the catch? There must be something bad about it, right? In reality, there isn't. It's just a different way of living your life and making money. You'll have more time to spend with family and friends because you don't need to work long hours anymore. Imagine what it would be like to sit back and relax while the cash comes rolling in! Who wouldn't want that?

This is possible. We've proven it for ourselves and for the hundreds of happy, fully satisfied clients we serve. There's nothing wrong with making money. The only thing that can happen is that you might make a lot more of it than before!

Don't believe me? Keep reading and keep learning as you continue on your path to success. You'll be surprised at what you find when we get done here.

We've been living this way for years and we know firsthand how beneficial the system has been for us personally, professionally, financially, and emotionally. It's not hard — and in fact, it will feel like something that was missing from your life all along because once everything clicks into place there are no limits to what can be accomplished or achieved. Just imagine having enough time to spend with family and friends while still being able to take care of everything else that is going on.

- **Work from home instead of going to the office.** One of our clients, John, recently said this, "I was tired of my 9 to 5 job. I felt like I was wasting my life away sitting in an office, never being able to spend time with my family and friends because I'm always working. But you know what? Things changed when I discovered Residual Income Magic and followed Brycen's and Jerrika's advice. Now I'm making more money than ever before!"
So don't get discouraged. The world is changing and there are many new opportunities for people like you and me so you can finally take control of your life again. Look, we only

go through life once. It is so important to spend quality time with your loved ones and to do something that you love. That's what's happened to me and some days I have to pinch myself in disbelief.

- **Retire early with no worries**. "In its new U.S. Retirement Survey, New York-based global asset management company Schroders found that just 26% of Americans near or at retirement age (ages 60 to 67) have enough money saved for retirement."[8] Many people who retire end up running out of money before they run out of life.[9] They are stuck in a cycle where they can't enjoy their retired life because they don't have the financial means to do so. This is the main reason why many people who reach retirement age, especially if it's unexpected, struggle with being able to afford day-to-day living expenses and medical emergencies without outside help from family members or friends.

The lack of planning for retirement can leave you feeling like you're no longer in control and struggling with feelings of fear, guilt, shame, or embarrassment concerning your finances. I can't tell you how many times I've been asked this question: "What's it like to retire early with no financial worries?"

Well, the truth is that there are many different ways to go about retiring. There are those who work hard and save for years until they're finally able to kick back and relax. And then there are those who have just enough money saved up from their 9 to 5 job that they don't need a second source of income, which means no more waking up at 6 am every day!

That sounds amazing doesn't it? But what does retirement really entail? What do you do with all your time now that you're not working anymore? How do you get through the days without having any obligations or deadlines looming. And what if you had so much money for retirement that you spent your time whenever you wanted just watching that money grow even more. That would be a nice problem to have, would it not?

- **Feel great about helping support family members, kids, and grandparents.**

Who can live the residual income lifestyle? Can anyone do it? If so, how?

"Whatever your mind can conceive and believe, it can achieve."
— *Napoleon Hill*

There are thousands of people who want to quit their jobs and live the residual lifestyle, but they don't know how. They think that it is impossible for anyone with kids, a mortgage or other responsibilities to make enough money online. Not only can you succeed in making residual income online but your success might even exceed your expectations.

Here's a true story about one of our clients: Danny Allen, for example is 34 years old and worked for USAA for 10 years topping out at $49,000. After spending the last three years exclusively living off passive income streams he now has a net worth of over $2 million.

Here's why anyone can live the residual income lifestyle through the Internet:

- **You can start with very little money.** We're living in a time when the world is changing faster than ever before. Technology is progressing at lightning speed, and it's giving people more freedom to live their lives the way they want. It's also making it easier for entrepreneurs to make money online while working from home, often without investing a ton of money. How much you invest in starting a business and the type of business you pick is up to you. You'll learn more about this as we share what we've learned — so keep reading.

- **You don't need a degree to succeed.** No one is going to hand you a degree. It's not for sale, and there are no shortcuts. But, this doesn't mean that people without a college education can't be successful with an Internet business. On the other hand, I've never seen someone succeed with an online business who didn't have the drive and ambition to make it happen. And guess what? As the author of this book, I still don't have a college degree — but look at my success. By the way, what you'll get from me is not a college degree, but you will receive what many have called a degree in how to succeed on the Internet.

- **The Internet is always on and you can work 24/7.** This means that you can be making money while you sleep.

Furthermore, Internet is available almost everywhere too, making it possible to work from almost anywhere.

You may be asking, "How does this work?" Well, there are affiliate programs where we can earn commissions on other people's products or services without having any inventory.

"Sounds interesting! Do you have an example?" One opportunity we help many of our clients with is selling on Amazon. We do all the work for them. Stay tuned to learn more about this later in the book.

- **You'll be able to create your own schedule and work at your convenience**. This flexibility makes it easier for you to make money. You can log in to your account at any time of day or night. You can do what you need to do when you want to do it with the kind of flexibility that is unlike any 9 to 5 job. I get excited for you every time I think about this.

- **You don't need to be an expert in online marketing**. There are step-by-step guides as well as complete done-for-you solutions available. In fact, and this may surprise you depending on your needs, we have one solution that makes it so you don't have to do anything. We do all the work for you with success guaranteed. I'm serious. You'll learn more about this later in the book as well.

- **You can work as little or as much as you wish**. You work when you want to work or can do a minimal amount of work if you pick a system in which someone else does the work for you.

Henry Ford, the man who revolutionized the automobile industry, once said, "Whether you think you can, or you think you can't, you're right."[10] You CAN achieve success in making an ongoing life-changing stream of residual income from the Internet.

How to decide if the residual lifestyle is right for you

"You can change direction if you feel like you have missed your way... Decide to do that now! Go back a little more and begin from where you missed out! If only you are ready to rise again, you can make a right decision in that tight belly of the shark. Jonah did that earlier!"

— Israelmore Ayivor

It's not always easy to make the decision about whether or not you should start making money online. There are so many opportunities out there that it can be overwhelming and hard to figure out which one is right for you. Below are some questions and other thoughts to help you decide if the residual income lifestyle, earning money from the Internet, is right for you and what type of opportunities you might want to pursue:

- **How much time do I have?** The truth is, the average person spends more than two hours a day commuting to and from work. That's 10 minutes per mile (round trip) spent in the car or on public transportation for every hour spent at work. If you're like most people who spend 45 minutes driving each way to and from work, that means it can take up to as much as four hours of your 8-hour workdays just going back and forth! This doesn't include any time lost due to traffic jams or accidents — so we have another few hours there depending on where you live. Imagine what you could do with that many hours if you went full time with an Internet business! If you want the Internet business as only a side hustle there are solutions for that as well. Later, I'll tell you about one option where it takes little of your time because we do all the work for you.

- **What kind of work makes me happy?** I don't know your situation, of course, but most of us have the same basic things that make us happy. Here's what I've heard from others about why having an Internet business with an ongoing stream of residual income makes them happy:

  ✓ **Financial freedom.** If you get an expert to make sure you do it the right way, you'll be very happy with your finances because it's possible that the Internet can give you all the income you would ever want.

  ✓ **The ability to sleep in with no worries.** Some days many of us love to sleep late. With an Internet business, sleeping late whenever you want isn't an issue. Why? Because while you sleep your Internet business is working it's mojo bringing you new business and new customers. What could be better than that?

  ✓ **You can work your own hours.** Want to go to the beach right now? No problem. Want to visit a friend right now? No problem! Want to take a vacation? No problem! You get the idea!

✓ **The end of yelling.** Your boss won't yell at you because you won't have one. I don't know your wife, if you have one, but it will be hard for her to yell at you about finances if you keep raking in the cash, right?

- **How serious am I about starting a business?** Yes, you have to be focused and a bit intentional and serious (although not too much). In fact, having an Internet business does not need to be a serious business. In fact, the more ridiculous and outlandish you are on social media or in person, the better off you're going to be come retirement time. The trick is that for every 10 hours of work, you need to spend three hours doing something else.

- **Am I willing to learn enough skills in order for me to succeed in this industry?** Wait, strike that question. Why? Because if you don't want to spend time learning, we'll do the whole thing for you. Or, we have a way you can take the slower learning path.

- **Do I have any other income streams that could provide any needed investment money to start making money online?** This is a great question. However, we have a way for most people to succeed, even if money is a bit of an issue.

Only you can decide if the residual lifestyle is right for you. If it is and you have the right tools, information, and guidance, then you can get ready to start living a spectacular life.

Advantages of a residual lifestyle

"Some people want it to happen. Some wish it would happen. Others make it happen."

— Michael Jordan

If you're tired of your 9 to 5 job and just want a way out, then we have some good news for you. There are many advantages to earning income online instead of working 9 to 5. You can work from home, set your own schedule, and work as much or as little as you want! All it takes is a few minutes each day and you'll be on your way up the ladder in no time flat. Check out these advantages of making money online!

- **Flexibility**. The beauty of making money online is that you can do it anytime and anywhere — even in your pajamas! Whether it's 10 pm on a Friday night or 8 am on a Monday morning, as long as you have Internet access, then you can make money.

- **There's no commute**. You can just log in anytime and pick up where you left off. What do you think of when you hear the words "commute to work?" Do you immediately feel tired and drained? This may be because commuting is one of the most common causes of stress. When people are commuting, they are stuck with their own thoughts, which can lead to worry and anxiety about other aspects in life. If that doesn't sound like a great way to start your day, consider this: not having a commute could actually make your life better! Read on for more information about how being able to work from home can improve your quality of life.

- **You can set your own hours.** Just take a break when life gets too busy or stay up late working on an important project if that's what you *want* to do. The importance of taking several days off from work should not be underestimated. If you're looking for a way to rejuvenate your mind, body, and soul, then it's time for you to take some time off. Having an Internet business lets you take a break at any time. There are many benefits that come with taking time off such as improved creativity, increased energy levels, and less stress.

- **You can work from any location.** Coffee shops are always nice, but there are also plenty of "co-working" spaces. Top-ranked motivational speaker Tony Robbins has said, "What is great about being able to work from anywhere? You have the ability to live your life and explore new places without having to worry about how it will affect your job."[11]

- **You are not depending on one source of income.** You don't have to depend solely on your current job as a source of income. If you were to lose your job, you wouldn't lose everything and you would have an additional way to pay for any unexpected emergencies

- **You can pick an area that you enjoy.** You won't be forced to accept a job you may not like but have to take because of the money you need to make.

- **You would have the ability to ramp up your income.** If

your life situation changes and you need additional income, you will have it. In a fixed-pay job, such an opportunity simply does not exist. Everyone is looking for a way to make some money in this tough economy. You've may have been told that the best way to do so is by starting your own business. However, most of us are not entrepreneurs and we don't have the time or resources to start something from scratch. What if I told you there is an easier solution?

- **If you're tired of working for someone else, then it's time to explore online opportunities!** A good internet business can in effect print money for you while giving you more free time than any other type of opportunity out there! It doesn't matter where you live — as long as there's a reliable high speed connection, an Internet business is perfect for anyone who wants some extra cash and more spare time. How are you able to "print" money? All you need is a business that attracts people with a compelling offer and a reason for them to buy and they will pull out their credit card. If you need more money you just use our proven way to get more people to buy. If you want, we'll even do all that for you as well.

Disadvantages of residual lifestyle

"Worrying is using your imagination to create something you don't want."

— *Abraham Hicks*

Although earning money online may seem like an ideal situation, like every other opportunity there are some disadvantages that you need to be made aware of. These disadvantages are:

- It will take some time on your part to manage an online business unless you pick a done-for-you option or someone else does all the work for you. We do done-for-you if that solution is right for you.

- Some type of investment on your part will be required to get started earning residual income online. It will either be an investment of time, an investment of money, or an investment of both. Although making money online can be relatively easy it is not a magic pill where are you simply click a button and start making money right away. Wondering if you have the money to invest if you need to invest money based on what you picked? We'll show you a proven shortcut to solving that problem.

- You could actually lose money in an online marketing effort if you don't have the right information and right direction. Although not as bad, you could end up putting in a lot of time and effort and not making any money. There are thousands and thousands of people in the world who have tried to make money online and have not made dollar one. This does not mean you cannot do this but you do require the right information so that you can succeed. We have all the information you need that has worked for hundreds of people. Some are making hundreds of thousands of dollars a year.

- There's a risk of being scammed. There are many scams out there, so make sure you follow these tips on how to avoid them: do your research before investing money in any company; ask questions about the company's products or services such as how much does it cost, where can I buy it from etc.; find out if they have a refund policy before signing up for anything; and always read reviews about their product or service first. This will save you a lot of headaches later!

- It takes a lot of time to make money online. This is a common belief but, if you pick the right opportunity, it takes less time than you think.

- You have no guarantee that you'll ever make any money. This is another false belief as far as we are concerned. One of our highly successful Internet marketing business opportunities provides a complete money-back guarantee.

Exercises

"Since everything is a reflection of our minds, everything can be changed by our minds."

— *Gautama Buddha*

Here are some questions for you to reflect on to make sure that you understood what you're reading and to help you decide if the residual income lifestyle is for you:

- What could be the key benefits to you of living the residual income lifestyle?

- What disadvantages do you see in living the Internet residual income lifestyle?

- Do you think you can succeed at this? If so, why?

- Are you afraid that you may fail at this? If so, why?

- If you could wave a magic wand for turning the dream of ongoing residual income into a reality, what would it look like after the wand was waved?

- What could be the key benefits of living the residual income lifestyle?

CHAPTER 3
TURNING YOUR DREAM OF RESIDUAL INCOME INTO A REALITY

"Don't let your dreams be dreams."

— Jack Johnson

In this section of the book we share some specific steps you can take to turn your dreams of residual income into a reality.

A plan to get you there:
Steps to success

"By failing to prepare, you are preparing to fail."

— Benjamin Franklin

So, now that you've made it this far in the book you're probably wondering, "Now what do I do?" Here are some steps to help get you started:

- Decide if the residual lifestyle is definitely for you.

- Decide what you are willing to do and not willing to do to achieve this dream.

- Decide what you are looking for before you pick specific opportunities to explore.

- Decide how much money and time you are willing to invest to live the dream life.

- Prepare a list of questions to help you analyze which opportunity is right for you.

- Pick an expert who walks his talk and has had success with residual income. Meet with him and get his advice.

- Based on your meeting, decide on your personal direction.

- Decide on the timeframe to start your residual income business.

- If you plan to leave your job, first develop a plan to leave and then do it!

- Take massive action to achieve your dreams.

Within this section of the book I will provide you with a list of suggestions concerning what to look for in an opportunity, questions to ask, and other helpful tips and techniques.

What to look for in an opportunity

"If somebody offers you an amazing opportunity but you are not sure you can do it, say yes – then learn how to do it later."

– *Richard Branson*

Here are some questions to help you decide what to look for:

- Are others having proven, indisputable success with this opportunity?

- Is there a real consumer demand for what you would be offering? How do you know?

- Is this opportunity focused on a fad or a trend that may go away fairly quickly?

- Is this opportunity so new that it is unproven?

- Is this opportunity something I could personally get excited about?

- If I am working and plan to use this as additional income can I realistically do the work that is required? Or can I hire someone to do the work for me?

- Can I easily scale and grow this opportunity?

- How much time will it take to learn how to do this if I want to do it myself?

- Does this opportunity match my desires in terms of lifestyle?

- How long will it take to earn the first dollar?

- How long will it take to reach my financial goals with this opportunity?

- What are the advantages and disadvantages of this opportunity?

- Are there any guarantees with this opportunity?

- Can I easily sell this business to someone else if and when I want to do that?

- Is the opportunity sustainable?

- With your approach to the opportunity you are considering, are you in total compliance with terms of service?

Questions to ask a consultant or anyone offering you a program

"In the old economy, it was all about having the answers. But in today's dynamic, lean economy, it's more about asking the right questions. A more beautiful question is about figuring out how to ask, and answer, the questions that can lead to new opportunities and growth."

— *Eric Ries*

So, you are thinking about pursuing the residual lifestyle by starting an Internet business? If you're like most people, making a decision about what to do and how to do it can be overwhelming. You may be concerned that you don't know the right questions to ask. The right questions can help you avoid common mistakes and find just the right opportunity to meet your needs by providing a constant and never-ending stream of residual income month after month.

Here are some key questions for which you need to get answers as to whether you will be doing your own research about an opportunity or should you ask someone you may hire to help you make the decision.

- How long have you been involved in this field?

- Please provide four references I can contact.

- Has anyone stopped working with you, and if so, why?

- Why should I utilize you to help me?

- What are your strengths and weaknesses when it comes to you helping me?

- Please describe exactly what you do to help me initially launch this business

- Do you provide ongoing support and what does that support entail?

- What times of day and what days of the week are you available?

Questions to ask about the opportunity itself

- Is this opportunity something that I can see myself being a part of over the long term?

- What is my investment and how much do I need to invest each month?

- What is my total initial cost to get involved and when do I pay?

- Is there an ongoing cost, and if so, how much is it?

- Do you provide a no-questions-asked money-back guarantee? What are the terms of the guarantee?

- Have you addressed any FTC (Federal Trade Commission) requirements if there are any, and if so, how?

- Are there any questions that I should ask that I have not?

- What is your reputation on the Internet?

- Are you registered with any business associations? Which ones?

Mistakes to avoid when investigating and starting an online Internet business

Many people are looking for a way to make money online, but they end up making mistakes that cost them both time and money. The Internet is flooded with business opportunities that promise you huge profits if you just pay their monthly fee or buy their expensive training course. They promise the world and never deliver on those promises. We have been running an Internet business for over 10 years now and we have learned from our own mistakes as well as from seeing what other successful entrepreneurs do right when it comes to building a profitable online business. Here are some mistakes to avoid and if you follow this advice, it will increase your chances of success:

- Being misled into thinking that you can begin making money immediately from an online program. Most programs take a bit of time and patience

- Not being realistic about the amount of time it takes to successfully earn money online

- Picking a program in which you cannot realistically spend the time required to get the results you want

- Being fooled into believing that you can succeed on the internet without investing money in an internet business

- Buying into a program where there is no money-back guarantee

- Not doing your own research to check out the opportunity and see the reputation of the people involved

- Not looking for information that shows how others have succeeded in making residual income online from the opportunity that you are investigating

- Being unrealistic about the amount of money you will make and how long it will take to make it

---

Critical success factors for a successful residual income-generating Internet business

When it comes to success in business and in life, it's important to know about critical success factors. Critical success factors are areas that are vital to the success of a business or an individual.

Keep these critical factors in mind when pursuing residual income online and your probability of success will greatly increase:

- You need to have a clear goal and strategy for your business.

- Be aware of the competition in your field and how they are doing it better than you.

- It is important to stay current with technology, because the industry changes rapidly.

- Always be ready to adapt — change is inevitable.

- Keep an eye on trends while staying true to yourself.

- Make sure that you are tracking all of your stats so that you can see what is working and what is not.

Exercises

The previous section contained critical information about how to turn your dream into a reality. Since this is critical information, below are some review questions. If you don't remember an answer, then just read this section again.

- What are the critical steps in a plan to successfully get an ongoing stream of residual income?

- What are important questions to ask when considering a residual income opportunity?

- What questions would you ask someone who offers to be your consultant who is helping you succeed in getting a residual income opportunity that really works for you?

- How would you go about investigating a potential opportunity? What would you do and what questions would you ask?

- What are the key mistakes you should avoid in moving forward to earn a successful residual income stream?

CHAPTER 4
OPPORTUNITIES AND RECOMMENDATIONS

Have you ever wondered what Internet business opportunities exist and which one you should pick for your residual income stream? In this section, we will give you examples of various opportunities. After years of experience trying to figure this out for ourselves, we will also share our recommendations including our top one.

Examples of Internet Business Opportunities

There are hundreds of opportunities for starting an Internet business, with some of them providing an ongoing stream of residual income. One key question you need to decide is what type of business is right for you. Below are some examples of the types of Internet businesses you could consider with our recommendations for what opportunities you should consider more closely.

- **Creating and selling information products online**. The information publishing business is huge because many

41

people are searching for information. With selling information products, you have to do all the work, including marketing. It can be difficult to find a niche that is profitable. The competition online can be fierce. Creating products takes time and effort — it's not easy money. One critical component is driving traffic to the location where you are selling these products. To do this will take either time or money — time if you are going to use organic traffic. Organic traffic is created by developing content that will rank high in the search engines. This usually takes time. All the hard work can be destroyed if the search engines change their algorithms.

- **Develop an email newsletter**. People such as Ben Settle have made substantial money from having an email newsletter, but it takes a lot of effort. First, you need the time to create compelling newsletter content on an ongoing basis. Second, you need a strategy to continually build your email list. This takes time and effort. Content must be continually generated and the list must be built on a continual basis since people do unsubscribe.

- **Creating and maintaining a membership site**. People do make money from membership sites, but this is also a lot of work. You have to put in a lot of hard work and time. In addition, it can be difficult to make money from your membership site at first. Your site could get hacked or compromised, leading you to lose all of your data. If you are not good with computers, it will be challenging for you to create your own website. You will probably need to hire someone to do this, which is an added cost. You could learn to do it yourself, but that takes time. It is also possible that other people will copy the idea behind your membership site and take over the market share before you do. There's always a chance that someone else has already created a similar membership site as yours so there would be no point in creating one yourself.

- **Selling website services to local businesses**. There still is huge demand for websites since many businesses do not have an online presence. The competition is fierce and there are a lot of fees involved. You need to be tech savvy and have knowledge about different platforms, or you need to hire full-time employees or outsource to those who do this. This involves managing others, which can sometimes be challenging. Also it's not always easy to get your foot in the door with local business owners.

- **Setting up an Internet marketing agency to help businesses market online.** There's a huge need for helping businesses to market online. There are many components to this such as Facebook advertising, Google advertising, business listings and more. It takes a lot of time to build the business. You have to take on more responsibility than you would at an established company. Also, there are risks associated with being self-employed, such as not having any job security or benefits. Your success is dependent on how much effort you put in and what kind of skills you bring to the table. Marketing agencies that service larger companies will always be more desirable employers because they offer stability and better pay. Setting up your own Internet marketing agency means taking on all the risk without any of the benefits (i.e., health insurance, paid vacation days, etc.).

- **Selling stock photos online.** If you enjoy taking photos, stock photos can be a good passive income source for you. Through stock photography websites such as Shutterstock (and there are many others), you can earn money by selling your photos online. Photos can be in any niche that interests you, such as travel, food, or sports. As an independent photographer, you can sell your images on various stock photography websites. If you are a photographer, this would be an enjoyable business for you to work in. However it takes time to drive people to your site to see the photos and it is sometimes difficult to know in advance what people will buy.

- **Becoming a social media marketing consultant.** Social media is huge these days and many businesses do not know how to market in this important way. Social media marketing consultants are often expected to work long hours. Social media is always changing, so you need to be constantly on top of trends. Competition is intense in this field. You can quickly and easily lose a client. And, it can be difficult to get started in this field without experience or connections — this also takes time and effort There is no guarantee that a consultant will always be busy enough to make a living wage.

- **Recommended by Wifi wealth:** *Turning YouTube into a "Cash Cow" (this is a new program we just launched).* With our help on a done-for-you basis, you can become a "YouTube Cash Cow." A YouTube Cash Cow is a person who has found success on YouTube by gaining audiences for their videos and then monetizing them. More than $34 billion in advertising revenue in three years: Creators finally know how much money YouTube makes, and they want more of it.[12] With over 1 billion users worldwide, there are many ways to generate profit from this site — from ads shown before your videos to sponsored content in your video descriptions or even creating products that will be sold through your channel page.[13] Ask us if you'd like to learn more about this exciting new program.

Here's what you get:

- ✓ You can become a highly successful Youtuber with hardly any work

- ✓ All the necessary materials and tools to be successful

- ✓ A large audience from YouTube's one billion users worldwide

- ✓ Ongoing monetization once you reach the level of at least 4,000 subscribers

- ✓ A loyal audience for your YouTube Videos

- ✓ More money on sponsored content in your videos

- ✓ Passive income with a YouTube "Cash Cow"

✓ Never having to worry about monetization again — we'll take care of that for you

- **Recommended by Wifi Wealth:** *Instagram Influencer and Profit Magic*. If you're wondering why leveraging the power of Instagram is a smart decision, the facts are clear. You have an opportunity to tap into a large audience. You can get a large follower count, which gives you instant influence/credibility which will open doors to people/places/opportunities that would not otherwise be available to you. There are over one billion monthly active users and 500 million daily active users.[14] You get access to a prime audience for marketers — 35 years old and younger. You get a great opportunity to increase a business's reach because 50% of Instagram users follow at least one business. According to Omniscore, 200 million Instagram users visit at least one business profile per day.[15] You get more interactions. Instagram generates 4x more interactions than Facebook.[16] More interactions means more exposure and better results. You get access to power users. Power users (30k-500k followers) make an average of $775 for an Instagram video, $507 for an image post and $210 for a story.[17]

With our Instagram program, we give you a guaranteed number of followers based on your requirements. We do this by leveraging the marketing power and influence of our high profile connections. We also create your online brand, teach you how to monetize Instagram, and give you both time freedom and a clear path to the lifestyle you want. We also provide regular updates.

Our top recommendation: Amazon FBA by Wifi Wealth

Harness the money generating power of the largest online marketplace in the world — Amazon

A Shortcut to Proven Success

After spending eight years in the Internet marketing business and testing many different approaches and models for residual income success, the one we like the most is Amazon FBA — if done in the right way. FBA (Fulfillment By Amazon) is a service that provides storage, packaging, and shipping assistance to sellers on Amazon. Sellers are relieved of many of the burdens and given more flexibility in their selling practices as a result.

The benefits of selling through Amazon FBA are many. They include:

- Amazon is one of the most stable, established, fast-growing, and successful digital marketplaces in the world. Amazon sales continue to grow exponentially. During one quarter in 2021, daily sales were $1.2 billion. As Amazon grows, you can grow too.[18]

- There is no need to pay for traffic and spend a ton on advertising. Amazon does the advertising for you.

- One in five (19%) makes $25,000-$250,000/month, amounting to annual sales between $300,000 and $3,000,000; another 6% make more than $250,000 in monthly sales.[19]

- Making money on Amazon is proven to work. Amazon sellers see relatively high profit margins. More than ⅔ of sellers (68%) are earning profit margins higher than 10%, and 36% of sellers are earning profit margins above 20%.

- Amazon is here for the long term. You don't have to worry about an online profit-generating presence suddenly closing and leaving your residual income source only a past dream.

Disadvantages of having an Amazon FBA store

- Picking a winning product is difficult.

- It is difficult to get a high ranking (on the first two pages of Amazon) for your products. If people don't see your products you will never sell them.

- There's no guarantee you'll succeed after investing a lot of time and money learning, setting up and managing your Amazon presence

- Sourcing products takes time and expertise.

- It is almost impossible to source products that have high margins.

- Your listing on Amazon can be hijacked and used by others.

- Implementation timeframe to set up a store can be long

- Extensive time is required to manage your store. For example, you have to manage inventory, customer support, reviews, etc.

Our Top Recommendation: Wifi Wealth's "Powered By Amazon FBA System"

Here at Wifi Wealth, we've created a program that fully leverages the benefits of Amazon FBA while successfully overcoming any disadvantages. After more than five years of developing and refining our system, we're now helping hundreds of people worldwide enjoy an amazing residual income lifestyle using Amazon FBA — our "Powered by Amazon FBA System."

When you partner with us using this revolutionary system we:

- Provide a done-for-you service where you sell products on Amazon, the largest online marketplace in the world.

- Optimize your listing for maximum traffic so you get seen by your target audience.

- Provide you with product recommendations using our proprietary product analysis and evaluation tool.

- Trademark your brand.

- Create a private label product.

- Guarantee adherence to Amazon rules so you don't risk getting closed.

- Leverage our relationship with our suppliers so you get the best margin.

- Handle all fulfillment and manage the inventory.

- Do all the work for you — it's a hands-off residual income source.

Here's what you get when you sign up for Wifi Wealth's Amazon program:

- Your own Amazon storefront

- Your own brand name

- Maximized product selection using our proprietary software

- A trademarked brand to prevent copycat competition

- Listing optimization so more buyers see your store and your product. We do this with our proprietary software.

- Hands-off customer service (you don't have to deal with customers)

- Complete inventory management including return handling

- Less risk of getting your storefront shut down because you don't have the professional knowledge you need for success

- No stress from having to do this while trying to balance other work and the other parts of your life

- Supplier relationships that would be difficult, if not impossible, for you to cultivate

- A money-back guarantee, a risk-free investment

Why You Owe It To Yourself to Explore This Opportunity from Wifi Wealth.

Here's what you get:

- You get an additional income stream without it costing you any time.

- You spend a minimal amount on advertising because you are leveraging your presence from the millions of dollars Amazon spends on advertising.

- You are working in the largest marketplace in the world and we do all the work for you.

- You leverage our supplier relationships giving you a larger profit margin.

- We do the work for you — it's a done-for-you solution.

- You get guidance from professionals who have managed millions of dollars in Amazon revenue for over fifteen hundred people.

CHAPTER 5
TIPS FOR FINANCIAL FREEDOM

"You can have a master's degree in making money, but you will still wind up broke if you have a PhD in spending it."

—Orrin Woodward

Financial freedom is something many people want but few obtain — even when it comes to retirement. In its new U.S. Retirement Survey, New York-based global asset management company Schroders found that just 26% of Americans near or at retirement age (ages 60 to 67) have enough money saved for retirement. Within that age group, 60% said they don't have enough saved for retirement, while 14% were unsure.[20]

You are probably imagining by now what it would be like to have the financial freedom that residual income could provide for you. When you gain this kind of income, how you manage it will make the difference between living a great life or a life of getting and then quickly lacking again. That's why I'd like to share how you can best manage your newfound wealth.

Did you know that the average lottery winner goes broke after just seven years. One key reason is that they don't know how to manage the newfound money.[21] The same could happen with an

Internet business. Here are tips for managing your wealth.

- Get accustomed to the idea of being wealthy.

- You can't spend more than you make.

- Make sure you save 10% of your earnings and give away another 10% to charity. The charitable act alone will make you feel even better about what you have accomplished.

- You need to invest money, but do research first.

- Donate some of what you earn — it's good karma.

- Meet monthly with an advisor who has knowledge about both personal finances and retirement plans — you don't want to retire broke!

- Think big picture, not short-term gain.

- Keep perspective on what's important in life.

- Stay open minded.

- Be grateful.

- Figure out how much money is coming in every month and figure out where it's going (tracking of spending habits).

- Create a budget - even if all your income comes from one source like investing or salary.

- Having fun with your newfound wealth matters, too!

- Expect some jealousy on the part of your friends. However, true friends will be totally happy for you and your new success.

CHAPTER 6
MOTIVATION MOJO

"To accomplish great things, we must not only act, but also dream, not only plan, but also believe."

— Anatole France

"Success is not final, failure is not fatal: It is the courage to continue that counts."

— Winston Churchill

"One day your life will flash before your eyes. Make sure it's worth watching."

— Gerard Way

I define "motivation mojo" as a quality to keep on keeping on until you've achieved your dreams. It's a combination of persistence, drive, a vision of what the future will be, and unwillingness to think "I can't do this." You can do it, just like I did and hundreds of other people have done after I have helped them.

Here are nine tips to help get and keep the "motivation mojo" needed to succeed:

1. Make a list of ten reasons why you will succeed and

review it at the start of each day. Post it on a wall where you can't avoid seeing it.

2. Create a dream book with photos of what the future will hold. Hold that vision in your head at least once a day. Imagine where in your head (right left center) it is and as you imagine, go to that place. Crazy, I know — but it works.

3. Get an accountability partner.

4. Monitor your mind chatter and shut it down if it does not support you.

5. Don't procrastinate. Get into action. Action gets results. Procrastination gets delay and slowness in getting to where you want to be.

6. Stay in the zone. Identify when and where you are most productive and work in that environment for best results. You're more motivated when in the zone.

7. Get enough sleep and eat healthy. Proper eating and sleep make a huge difference. Improper eating and sleeping are both mojo destroyers.

8. Take breaks so that you will come back refreshed.

9. Get quiet. If you're open to meditation do it. If you sometimes do it, make sure you do it every day.

CHAPTER 7
WIFI WEALTH CLIENT SUCCESS STORIES

Here are a few success stories from people who followed the advice provided by Wifi Wealth:

Wifi Wealth took my Amazon FBA business to the next level. Their ability to pick and source products has been a major factor. I was running an FBA store on my own before and doing just ok. I found Wifi Wealth after looking for some consulting to improve my business. However, after doing a few strategy sessions with them, I let them take over and run the store for me. It's been a great experience and I highly recommend them. **Chris S.**

Wifi Wealth catapulted my account from a few thousand followers to where I now have well over 100,000 followers. For me it was a no-brainer to work with these guys. I knew growing my followers was going to give me the influence I need to make even BIGGER moves! **Jeff S.**

When I started on my passive income journey, I was rather skeptical as I had tried other money-making programs in the past. The money-back guarantee they offered was what really made me 100% comfortable investing with them and trying again. And I can tell you wholeheartedly that putting my trust in Wifi Wealth was one of the best decisions I've ever made. I'm blown away on a daily basis that a company/program like this even exists. I cannot say enough nice things about the Wifi Wealth family! **Cindy M.**

When we started with Wifi Wealth around nine months ago, we had no idea how life-changing our decisions would be. Both myself and my husband work full-time and are raising two young kids so "getting ahead" seemed like a pipe dream. We were so wrong! Within six months, the hands-free, passive income we were making has opened up doors we never would have had access to previously. Thank you Wifi Wealth! You guys rock! **Gia A.**

CHAPTER 8

THE NEXT STEP TO SUCCESS

"The path to success is to take massive, determined action."
— Tony Robbins

There you have it — *Residual Income Magic*. Because you purchased this information, I want to do something special for you that we only do for our customers. And we're going to do this absolutely free.

We've created something called "The Financial Freedom Roadmap," along with a financial freedom coaching session. This session is a $397 value, but you get it FREE. We are so excited about what this will do for you.

Your roadmap and residual income magic coaching session is a breakthrough approach for living a dream life with no financial worries. With this guidance, you'll soon have the time and freedom to do everything you want to do — and more. *And* with less stress.

During this session, you'll discover seven steps for securing income on autopilot with all the work done for you — results guaranteed.

You're going to love what you'll learn from this seven-step roadmap. Furthermore, we'll share what keeps most people from achieving residual income on autopilot and exactly what to do differently so that success will be yours.

You'll also learn how to overcome the problem of not having enough time to work on making that residual income you desire. I know you are going to be blown away when you hear what this roadmap is about and how easy it is to get you the income you want. We understand where you are in life now, what you want for your life and how to secure your residual income as fast as possible.

Here's what one person had to say about our coaching session and roadmap:

> *I was amazed at how helpful the session and roadmap were. I got much clearer on exactly what needed to be done to earn residual income more quickly with less effort and less stress. I highly recommend that anyone thinking about earning residual income reserve a free session and get the roadmap.*

Whether you want to leave your 9 to 5 job, earn extra income on the side, or make more money as an entrepreneur, we're excited about how much we can assist you!

To book your session and get the roadmap, go to this web address:

www. wifiwealthway. com/appointments

Just imagine a future when you can look back on what getting this FREE book did for your life and your finances. The choice is yours.

Either just dream of residual income while never getting what you want or follow a proven autopilot path to residual income.

Here's to your success in living the life of your dreams,

Jerrika Cox

THANK YOU BONUS

As a thank you to anyone who purchased *Residual Income Magic*, I want to give you four free bonuses. If you have not yet received your bonuses, here is what you'll get:

Bonus #1

Special Report — 12 Wealth Management Success Secrets ($47 value): I love this bonus and only wish I knew what you'll know when you read this. You see, you cannot get a financially free life if you do not know how to manage your money. With this report, you'll know how to turn the ongoing stream of residual income you'll see into the lifestyle you've dreamed about.

Bonus #2

Special Report — 7 Profit Tips for Guaranteed Amazon FBA Success ($59 value): I can't wait for you to get this because it's one huge shortcut to residual income. When I first put this together I couldn't sleep because I was so excited about what it will do for people like you. You'll learn seven proven keys to successfully running your own Amazon FBA business.

Bonus #3

Instagram Insider's Secrets Report ($47 value): Discover how others have achieved massive success on Instagram. Learn how to get a large Instagram following, become a huge influencer and monetize your brand.

Bonus #4

Facebook Book Group Membership ($97 value): You get access to me and my private Residual Income Magic Facebook group with other people who have made the smart decision to get a copy of this breakthrough book. Here at Wifi wealth, we spend some of our days answering questions from current customers, and nowhere else online will you find this level of personal support for just getting this book.

To Get Your Free Bonuses, Go to this Address

www.wifiwealthway.com/bonuses

ABOUT WIFI WEALTH

Wifi Wealth helps people who want to leave their 9 to 5 jobs or earn a second income. For entrepreneurs already in business, WIFI helps them into the proven power of earning residual income from the Internet. In contrast to most residual income opportunity providers, we guarantee results or your money back. We also do all the work for you so you don't have to manage all the details. Our service is "done-for-you."

Co-founders, Brycen and Jerrika Cox

Brycen volunteering to help recovering alcoholics

As the founders of Wifi Wealth, we believe that nothing feels better than the comfort and security that comes from financial freedom. Our purpose in life is to help as many people as possible experience this freedom for themselves. The core objective of Wifi Wealth is to help others achieve financial independence through passive income, and thus attain comfort and security in life.

With over two decades of entrepreneurial experience between them, Brycen and Jerrika were determined to solve the number one problem that people face today: how to get ahead financially. In a time when it's becoming harder and harder just to get by, Brycen and Jerrika have concluded that this is where their own purpose in life can best be realized.

Jerrika volunteering at a local animal shelter

DISCLAIMER

Every effort has been made to accurately represent residual income opportunities as well as our products and their potential to help our customers, their businesses and/or their clients.

There is no guarantee that you will earn any money using the techniques and ideas in this book. Examples in the book are not to be interpreted as a promise or guarantee of earnings. Earning potential is entirely dependent on the person using our product, ideas, and techniques. We do not position any products or services as a "get rich scheme."

Any claims made of actual earnings or examples of actual results can be verified upon request. Your level of success in attaining the results claimed in our materials depends on the time you devote to the ideas and techniques mentioned, your finances, your knowledge, and various skills you may possess. Since these factors differ by individual, we cannot and do not guarantee your success or revenue generation, nor are we responsible for any of your actions related or not related to these materials.

Information in this book may contain information that includes or is based upon forward-looking statements within the understood meaning as of 2021. Forward-looking statements give our expectations or forecasts of future events. You can identify these statements by the fact that they do not relate strictly to historical or current facts. They use words such as "anticipate," "estimate," "expect," "project," "intend," "plan," "believe," and other words and terms of similar meaning in connection with a description of potential earnings or financial performance.

Any and all forward-looking statements in this book are intended to express our opinion of earnings potential. Many factors will be important in determining your actual results and no guarantees are made that you will achieve results similar to ours or anybody else's. No guarantees are made.

ENDNOTES

1 https://www.gartner.com/en/newsroom/press-releases/2019-10-29-gartner-says-only-13--of-employees-are-largely-satisf

2 https://www.usatoday.com/story/money/columnist/kay/2013/12/21/at-work-frustrations-inferiority/4117067/

3 https://dynamicsignal.com/2018/01/08/the-best-employee-engagement-statistics-you-should-know/

4 https://www.tonyrobbins.com/search/the+most+important+decision+you+will+ever+make

5 https://money.cnn.com/2017/07/12/pf/side-hustle/index.html

6 https://www.makingsenseofcents.com/2017/06/earn-extra-income.html

7 https://www.linkedin.com/pulse/power-residual-income-ben-stephenson/

8 https://www.valuepenguin.com/news/near-retirement-age-savings.

9 https://smartasset.com/retirement/average-retirement-savings-are-you-normal

10 https://www.goodreads.com/quotes/978-whether-you-think-you-can-or-you-think-you-can-t--you-re

11 https://www.statista.com/statistics/1122987/change-in-remote-work-trends-after-covid-in-usa/

12 https://www.theverge.com/2020/2/4/21121370/youtube-advertising-revenue-creators-demonetization-earnings-google

13 https://www.theverge.com/2020/2/4/21121370/youtube-advertising-revenue-creators-demonetization-earnings-google

14 https://www.oberlo.com/blog/instagram-stats-every-marketer-should-know

15 https://www.omnicoreagency.com/instagram-statistics/

16 https://adespresso.com/blog/instagram-statistics/

17 https://www.forbes.com/sites/jefffromm/2018/03/20/instagram-is-a-powerhouse-for-gen-z-influencer-marketing/?sh=71cb55681d64

[18] https://www.digitalcommerce360.com/article/amazon-sales/

[19] https://www.junglescout.com/blog/how-much-money-amazon-sellers-make/

[20] https://twitter.com/orrin_woodward/status/929890781128740864

[21] https://www.cnbc.com/2019/10/26/only-24percent-of-young-adults-are-financially-independent-by-22-per-pew.html

[22] https://www.careeraddict.com/why-motivation-is-important-for-success-and-happiness

Made in the USA
Columbia, SC
26 September 2022

67735569R00043